SOLO
Transport
Ships

Written and illustrated by

John Nicholson

SOLOS

Southwood Books Limited
4 Southwood Lawn Road
London N6 5SF

First published in Australia by Omnibus Books 2001
This edition published in the UK under licence from
Omnibus Books by
Southwood Books Limited, 2001.

This edition produced for The Book People Ltd.,
Hall Wood Avenue, Haydock, St Helens WA11 9UL

Text and illustrations copyright © John Nicholson 2001
Cover design by Lyn Mitchell
Typeset by Heidi Goeldi, Adelaide
Printed in Singapore

ISBN 1 903207 44 4

Contents

In 1492 an explorer named
Christopher Columbus crossed
the Atlantic Ocean. He sailed in
this tiny wooden ship, the *Nina*.

1

Big Ships

Do you ever go down to the docks to look at ships? They seem so big and solid, hardly moving as the water laps around them. It's hard to imagine them being tossed like corks by huge waves at sea.

Ships have been used to transport passengers and cargo for thousands of years. Long before planes were invented, people travelled across the sea in ships. They also sailed away in ships to explore the world.

Ships and boats often have girls' names. They are usually called "she". No one knows why.

Passenger Liner

Before air travel became cheap and easy, ships took passengers around the world. This American luxury liner was built in 1951. It sailed across the Atlantic Ocean, between America and Europe.

First class cabins are on the top level. Cheaper cabins (cabin class and tourist class) are lower down.

The North Atlantic is a cold ocean. A ship that is painted black stays warmer because black absorbs the heat of the sun. Closed-in decks keep out the cold.

This ship has lots of shops. It also has cinemas, restaurants and a swimming pool.

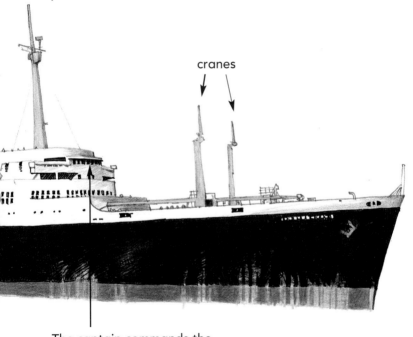

cranes

The captain commands the ship from the bridge. From here he can see a long way in all directions. The helmsman also stands here. He steers the ship.

Cruise Liner

This old cruise ship was built for use in the warmer parts of the world. Sunshine reflects off white, so the ship is painted white. This helps it to stay cool. The decks are open because people like to be outside in warm weather.

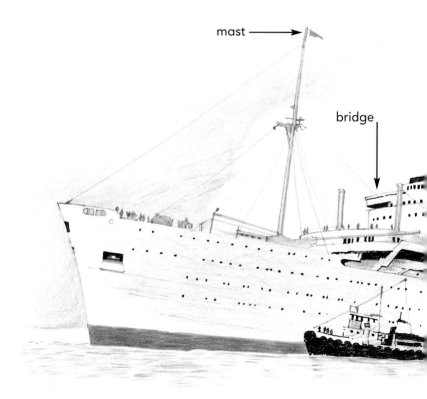

mast

bridge

The hull of the ship is divided into many watertight sections. If it gets a hole in it, only part of it will be flooded. This means the ship is less likely to sink. The hulls of all ships are made this way.

If the ship is in danger of sinking, there are lifeboats to carry the passengers and crew.

Big ships need tugboats to push and pull them gently into harbour (see pages 28-29).

Bulk Cement Carrier

This long, narrow ship was built for use on the canals of the Saint Lawrence Seaway in Canada. It carries up to 9,000 tonnes of bulk cement.

The cement is pumped out through these small openings. The hold can be emptied in less than 24 hours.

It is an old ship, powered by a coal-fired steam engine. Deep down in the engine room, three stokers shovel coal into the fires. Smoke, soot and heat make it hard to breathe.

Tanker

Oil tankers are the biggest ships afloat. Every year they carry billions of tonnes of oil all over the world.

Steel walls divide the oil storage space into lots of small tanks. The walls stop the oil sloshing from side to side as the ship rolls. Without them, the tanker could capsize (turn over).

Oil spilled from a damaged tanker spreads out over the sea. It kills many sea birds and animals.

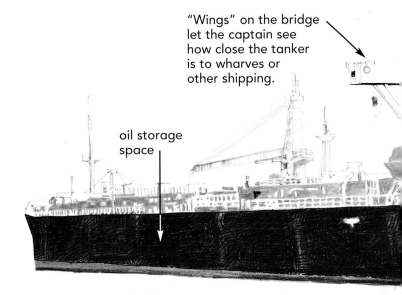

"Wings" on the bridge let the captain see how close the tanker is to wharves or other shipping.

oil storage space

The tanker's huge rudder *(left)* and propeller *(right)*. The rudder is used to steer the ship. The propeller pushes it through the water.

This is a very large ship, but it has only a small crew. Two lifeboats are enough to carry all the sailors. The boats are painted orange so they can be seen easily.

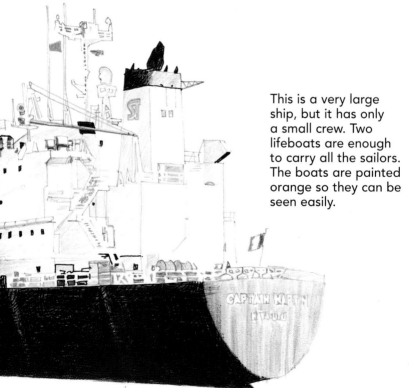

Cargo Ship

This cargo ship was not built to carry one kind of cargo. It can carry all sorts of things, from timber or tinned food to books or bales of wool.

A ship with no cargo is lighter and more likely to capsize. Sea water is pumped in to make it heavier. This extra weight is called ballast.

The engine room contains the main engine, a spare engine, pumps and diesel generators. The generators make electricity for light and heating.

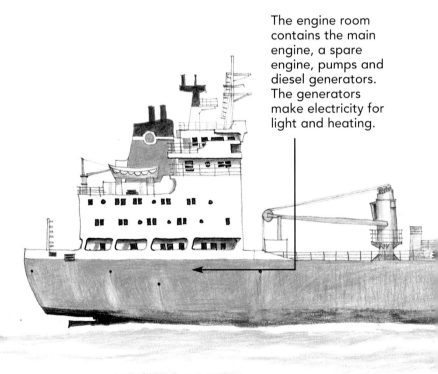

Pumps in the engine room pump out the ballast water when it is no longer needed. They also pump out water that has leaked into the bilges (the very bottom of the ship).

The strange shape of the bow (front) lets water flow past the moving ship more easily. It means the engines don't have to work so hard.

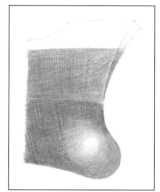

Cranes load and unload cargo.

Car Carrier

Some ships look more like huge floating boxes than ships. This one was built in 1994 for one purpose – to carry new cars and trucks. On each trip it carries about 2,000 cars from factories in Japan to Australia, New Zealand and other places.

There is a long, narrow door on each side of the car carrier. Cars can be driven straight out of the ship and on to the dock.

door

Floating Dry Dock

How do you get a big ship out of the water for painting and repairs?

First, water is pumped into tanks on each side of a floating dry dock. When the dock sinks, the ship can move into it. Now the water is pumped *out* of the tanks. As the dock floats, it carries the ship up with it.

2

Warships

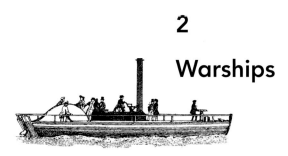

Until about fifty years ago, warships were built to be big and strong. Air warfare changed all that. War planes could easily attack and destroy these big, slow ships. Most warships are now made of lighter metals. They are small and fast.

The biggest naval ships built these days are aircraft carriers. They provide a landing strip for war planes. They also carry aeroplane fuel. In times of war, planes can operate a long way from home. They fly back to the carrier whenever they need to refuel.

Frigate

Frigates have many uses. They fight aircraft and submarines. They escort aircraft carriers and supply ships. They patrol coastlines. They can even help with ocean rescues.

The crew can seal off the inside of the frigate by closing all openings very tightly. In this way the ship can continue to operate during a nuclear war. A nuclear war could make the air poisonous to breathe.

Modern frigates have a thin steel or aluminium "skin". It makes them lighter, so they can move faster.

Radar and sonar equipment on the mast can find out if other ships or aircraft are near by.

The main gun fires 127mm diameter bullets. Frigates also carry anti-aircraft missiles.

Aircraft Carrier

An aircraft carrier is a floating runway.
Below the runway is the hangar (the
area where the planes are kept). Giant
lifts bring the planes up to the runway.

The runway is very short, so planes
need help to take off. A mechanical
arm called a catapult sticks up through
a slot. It pulls the plane very fast
along the runway and then lets it go.

When the plane is ready to land, a
hook on the aircraft grabs on to cables
stretched across the runway. They help
to slow the plane down.

The runway is
angled across
the deck.

With lots of planes taking off and landing, the deck gets very hot. It has to be cooled with water.

There is a small parking area for planes at the end of the carrier.

Mine-hunter

Mines are bombs. They float in the water to blow up enemy ships. Mine-hunters look for mines by using floating "robots" with searchlights and TV cameras. When they find a mine, they explode it.

The hull of a mine-hunter is made from fibreglass, not metal. Mines explode when metal objects come close to them.

Mine-hunters are also used for ocean rescues, Customs work (see pages 32-33) and coastal patrols. They usually carry anti-submarine weapons.

A mine, or floating bomb.

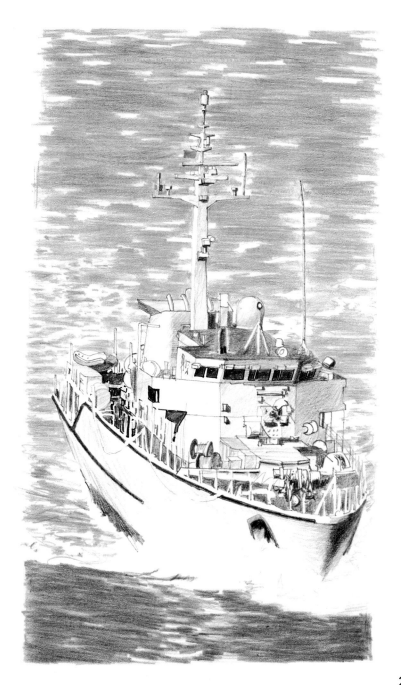

Submarine

Unlike other ships, a submarine works underwater. Its big ballast tanks are filled with water to make it sink. When the sub needs to surface, air is let into the tanks. The air forces the water out and the sub floats again.

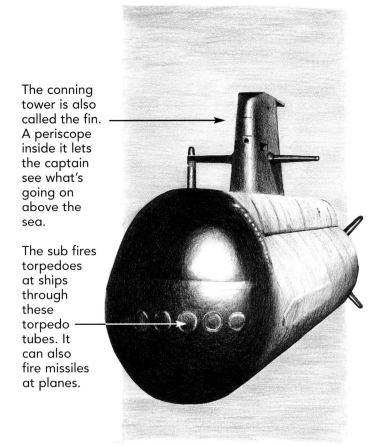

The conning tower is also called the fin. A periscope inside it lets the captain see what's going on above the sea.

The sub fires torpedoes at ships through these torpedo tubes. It can also fire missiles at planes.

3

Workboats and Special Ships

Ships and boats are used for many different kinds of work. Some of the most interesting are those built to do special jobs.

Some ships are made to carry just one sort of cargo. Others are used to explore the deepest parts of the sea. There are even ships that can break through ice.

Then there are ships that aren't really like ships at all. They don't float on water, but on air!

Tugboat

Most big ships have just one very big propeller and a rudder, both at the stern (back). They can't move into and out of small spaces by themselves. They need tugboats to help them.

Tugboats are small but very strong. They pull or push big ships into their berths at the wharf, or tow broken-down ships into harbour.

Rubber tyres pad the sides of the tug. They prevent damage to both the tug and the ship it is moving.

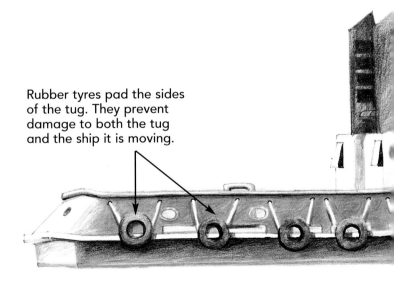

Most of them have fire-fighting equipment to put out fires on ships. They are also used to raise sunken ships or cargoes, and they help to clean up oil spills.

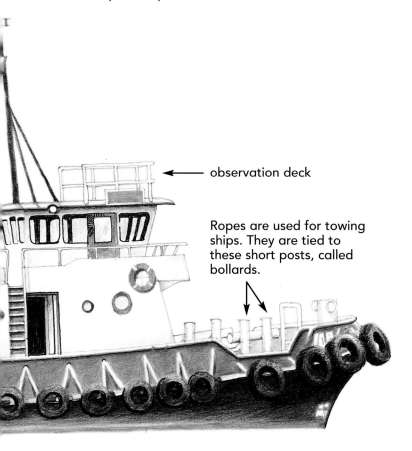

observation deck

Ropes are used for towing ships. They are tied to these short posts, called bollards.

Dredge

Floating dredges dig mud out of rivers and canals. They keep the shipping channels deep, so ships won't get stuck. Dredges are also used for mining. They dig up sand and gravel, and sometimes gold and silver, from river beds.

This bucket dredge is made up of two floats or pontoons. Between them is a moving chain of big steel buckets.

Every few minutes this winch moves the dredge along.

Chains are fixed to anchors to stop the dredge moving from side to side.

The buckets scoop up mud and tip it into a barge. When the barge is full, it is towed away to be emptied.

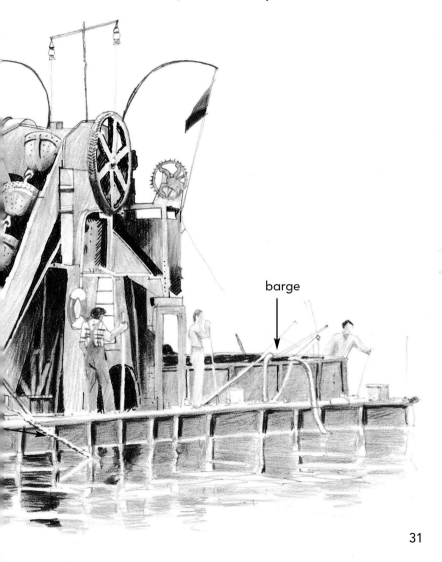

barge

Customs Boat

Customs officers are a special police force. It is their job to keep out people and goods that are not supposed to enter the country.

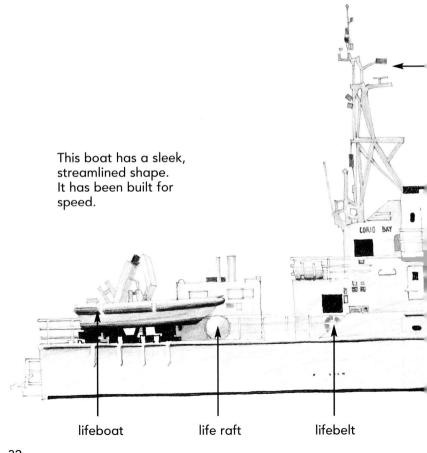

This boat has a sleek, streamlined shape. It has been built for speed.

CORIO BAY

lifeboat   life raft   lifebelt

Officers use fast patrol boats like this one to stop smugglers landing goods on lonely beaches. They also go out to inspect the cargoes of big ships when they come into port.

The mast holds navigation equipment (radar, sonar, radio aerials).

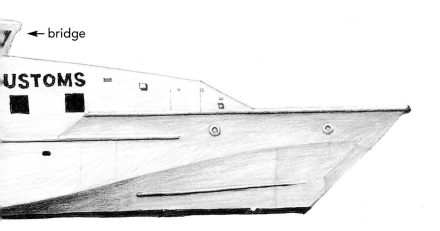

← bridge

USTOMS

Water Ambulance, Fire Tender

Some cities and towns have canals instead of roads. There are no cars, trucks, buses or delivery vans. Instead, there are many kinds of boats. Even the fire engines and ambulances are boats.

These two boats are from the city of Venice, in Italy.

In Venice, a fire engine looks like this.

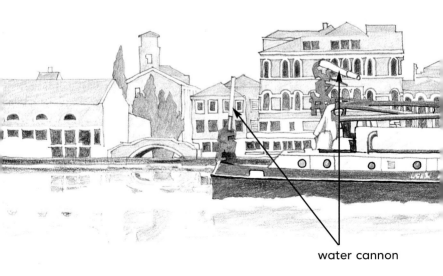

water cannon

In Venice, an ambulance looks like this.

Three water cannon can direct jets of water at a fire.

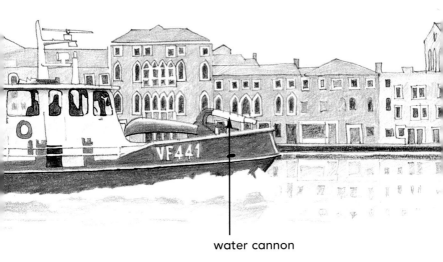

water cannon

Icebreaker

Near the North and South poles the ocean is often covered with a thick layer of ice. Ships used in these waters are called icebreakers. They have a strong, specially shaped bow that can break through ice.

This icebreaker carries amphibious vehicles. They can travel on water and land. They go through water like a boat, and across land (or ice) like a truck.

As the ship moves forward, its bow rises up onto the ice. The ice cracks and moves apart under its weight, and it settles down into the water again.

landing area for helicopters

Lightship

A lightship is a floating lighthouse. It has a very bright light to help ships' crews know where they are. Lightships also mark dangerous underwater rocks and sandbanks. They have saved many ships from running aground.

Very few lightships operate these days. Ships have satellite navigation systems to tell them where they are.

The lightship in this picture once marked a sandbank near the mouth of the River Thames in England. Its shape made it able to survive the roughest storms without rolling too much. Like all lightships, it is painted red. This makes it easy to see.

The light is mounted as high as possible. It can shine in all directions.

Davits raise and lower lifeboats.

Roll-on, Roll-off Ship

Container ships carry big steel boxes called containers. Using cranes, the containers are quickly unloaded off trucks or trains and on to ships.

The roll-on, roll-off ship makes loading and unloading even quicker.

A giant gateway and drawbridge in the stern (back) of the ship let trucks drive into the hold. When the ship is loaded, the drawbridge is closed tightly.

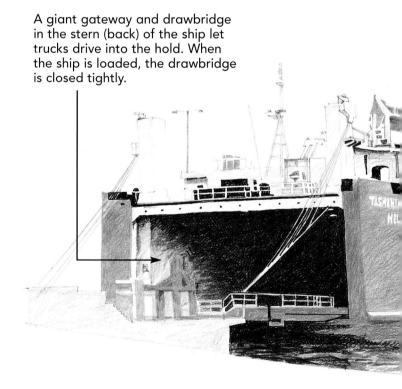

The ship backs into a specially built dock. The whole truck, with the container on it, can then drive straight into the ship's hold. The truck goes along for the journey as well!

Fishing Trawler

This is a wooden fishing trawler from Scotland. It tows a large bag-shaped fishing net along behind it. The fishermen pull in the net with a winch and empty the catch onto the deck. When the fish have been washed, they slide down a chute into the hold.

The trawl-winch pulls in the net when it is full of fish.

The boat stays at sea for three or four days at a time. It fishes in waters up to 160 kilometres away from its home port.

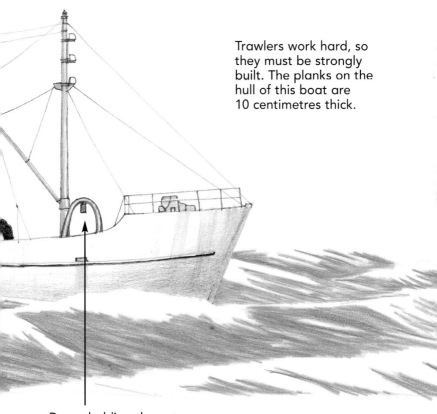

Trawlers work hard, so they must be strongly built. The planks on the hull of this boat are 10 centimetres thick.

Ropes holding the net pass through pulleys that hang from gallows.

Tramp Steamer

Tramp steamers are small, old cargo ships. Often they are near the end of their working lives. They go wherever they can find work to do.

Amidships (in the middle of the ship) are the bridge, the crew's cabins and the engine room.

cargo hold

This tramp works around the coast of Turkey and the eastern Mediterranean Sea. It carries things like coal, timber and bags of cement. The crew keep chickens on board to supply them with fresh eggs!

There are cargo holds fore (near the front) and aft (near the back).

cargo hold

Narrow Boats

The boats that travel along rivers and canals must be narrow, so they will fit between the banks. They must also be shallow, so they don't scrape along the bottom.

The long boats shown below carry cargo up and down the Rhine River in Germany. The boat at the bottom of the picture has a heavy load, so it is lying low in the water. There is no danger from big waves because rivers and canals are always calm.

The captain of this boat has brought his car with him!

This is a "delivery van" from Venice, where the streets are canals. When canals cross over each other, buildings that stand right on the water's edge can make it hard to see other traffic. Boatmen call out loudly to warn other boats that they are near.

Hovercraft

A hovercraft can travel on both water and land, but it doesn't float in water and it doesn't have wheels. It floats along on a thick layer of air held in by a sort of rubber skirt.

Big fans keep blowing air into the area under the boat.

Hovercraft don't need wharves. They simply sail up onto the beach to drop off passengers or goods. They are often used in the army and navy because they can go almost anywhere, very quickly.

This Canadian hovercraft is used all year round on lakes that freeze over in winter. It can travel at up to 150 kilometres per hour on water.

Hovercraft are pushed along by propellers, like those on small planes.

← rubber "skirt"

Underwater Research Vessel

Small submarines like this are used to explore the bottom of the ocean. They can dive to a depth of 10 kilometres. At this depth a normal submarine would be crushed by the weight of water. Underwater research vessels have walls up to 20 centimetres thick to cope with the pressure.

conning tower
(see page 26)

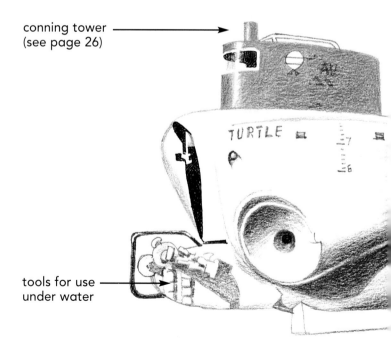

tools for use
under water

These little submarines do many other jobs, too. They are used to salvage cargoes from wrecked ships and make underwater repairs to dam walls and deep-sea oil rigs.

This American submarine was used to find an unexploded bomb in the Mediterranean Sea.

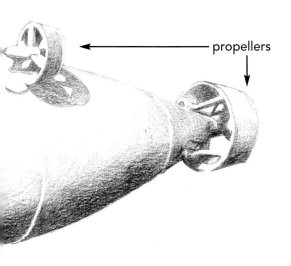

propellers

4

Ferries

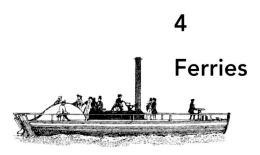

The first boats ever built were probably used to ferry people across rivers. Today millions of people go to work or school by ferry every day. These passenger ferries make lots of short trips from one side of a harbour or river to the other.

There are many kinds of ferries. Some are built to carry just a few cars and people. Others are as big as ocean liners. They carry cars, trucks and trains as well as people.

Big ferries can travel from island to island, or even from country to country.

Passenger Ferry

This is a commuter ferry. Like a train or a bus, it takes people to work and brings them home again at the end of the day. It doesn't go very fast. It stops at lots of little jetties along the way, picking up passengers and dropping others off.

There are seats inside, but many passengers like to stay outside on the deck.

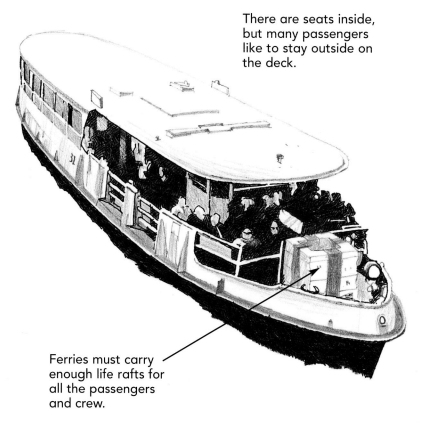

Ferries must carry enough life rafts for all the passengers and crew.

Quick-Cat

This ferry is a catamaran. It can travel longer distances and in rougher water than the ferry shown on page 53. It is also much faster.

This Quick-Cat is used by the army to carry troops.

A catamaran has two hulls instead of one, so it doesn't roll around much in rough seas. It is faster because less of the boat is in contact with the water. It is also totally closed in. There is no deck for passengers to stand on.

The catamaran's sleek, pointed shape helps it to go faster.

Hydrofoil

A hydrofoil is a boat that works like an aeroplane. Hydrofoils (wings) help it to "fly" through the water. When the boat is moving slowly, the hull floats in the water. When it starts to move faster, the hydrofoils make the hull rise up. With less water drag on the hull, the boat can travel very fast. A propeller pushes the boat along. It is on the end of a long shaft that comes from the engine.

The hydrofoils are under the water.

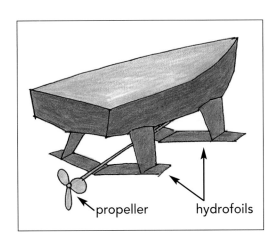

propeller   hydrofoils

This hydrofoil carries inflatable life rafts.

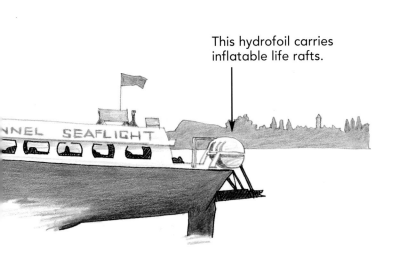

Car Ferry

Car ferries come in all shapes and sizes. This is a middle-sized one. It crosses the sea between Townsville (Queensland) and Magnetic Island, two kilometres away.

Like many ferries, this is an old military landing craft. It was built to sail right up to a beach and land army vehicles.

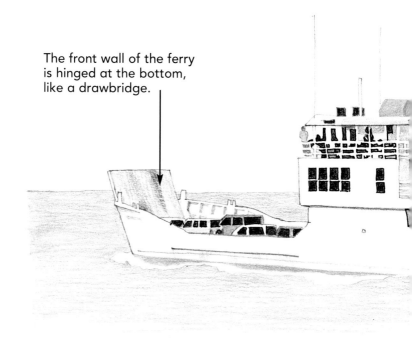

The front wall of the ferry is hinged at the bottom, like a drawbridge.

The front wall of the boat is lowered onto the beach and used as a ramp. Cars drive up the ramp and on to the ferry while the ferry is still floating in the water.

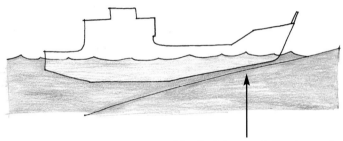

The hull is specially shaped so it can float in very shallow water.

Funnels and Flags

Ships' funnels are painted in all sorts of different colours and patterns. Each shipping company has its own colours, and its own special flag. Here are a few of them:

Australian National Line, Melbourne

Blue Star Line, London

Burns Philp (New Guinea), Port Moresby

Cunard Steamship Company, London

North Sea Ferries, Hull

Pakistan Shipping Corporation, Karachi

Ships also fly the flag of their home country.

Signal Flags

Before two-way radios were invented, ships' crews used signal flags to send messages. Each signal flag represents a letter or a number. It took a long time to send messages this way!

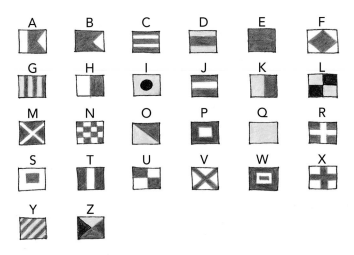

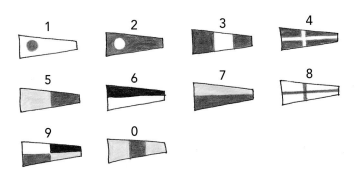

Glossary

barge ✳ A long, flat-bottomed boat for carrying loads on rivers or canals.

berth ✳ A ship's place at a wharf.

bridge ✳ The place where the captain and his officers control the ship.

canal ✳ An artificial (not natural) river or waterway that allows ships to travel inland.

cargo ✳ The load of things carried by a ship, train or aircraft.

commuter ✳ A person travelling to or from work.

dock ✳ A place where ships are loaded and unloaded.

drawbridge ✳ A big door or "gate" on a ship. It is hinged at the bottom and can be let down to form a "bridge" from the ship to the shore.

escort ✳ A ship travelling with another ship in order to protect it.

fibreglass ✳ Light, strong plastic made stronger by having glass fibres embedded in it.

gallows ✳ A frame on which something is hung.

hold ✳ The area inside a ship where the cargo is kept.

hull ✳ The main body of a ship or boat.

liner ✳ A ship that carries passengers along a regular route or line.

missile ✳ A small rocket that explodes when it hits its target. An *anti-aircraft missile* is aimed at aeroplanes.

navigation ✳ Working out where a ship is and which way it should go.

patrol ✳ To travel regularly around an area in order to protect it.

propeller ✳ A set of flat blades or arms spinning around a central shaft. The propeller makes a ship or aeroplane move forwards.

pump ✳ A machine for raising or moving water.

radar ✳ Using radio waves to find out where other ships are.

ramp ✳ A sloping floor or roadway that joins up two levels.

rudder ✳ A flat piece hinged to the back of a ship and used to steer it.

salvage ✳ To raise a sunken ship or its cargo.

satellite navigation system ✳ Using signals from a satellite to chart a ship's position.

smuggler ✳ Someone who brings goods into a country, against the law.

sonar ✳ Using sound (echoes) to find objects under water.

stoker ✳ A person who looks after the fires in the engine room of a steamship.

supply ship ✳ A ship used by the navy to carry food, fuel and other supplies.

torpedo ✳ An underwater missile that explodes when it hits a ship.

two-way radios ✳ Radios used by two people to talk to each other.

wharf ✳ A place where ships are loaded and unloaded, or lie at rest. See *dock*. (If there is more than one wharf, the word is *wharves*.)

winch ✳ A machine that uses a rope to lift or drag something. The rope is wound around a rotating drum.

Index